Limited Butterick Publishing Co.

Smocking, Fancy Stitches, and Cross Stitch and Darned-Net Designs

Limited Butterick Publishing Co.

Smocking, Fancy Stitches, and Cross Stitch and Darned-Net Designs

ISBN/EAN: 9783337255022

Printed in Europe, USA, Canada, Australia, Japan

Cover: Foto ©Andreas Hilbeck / pixelio.de

More available books at **www.hansebooks.com**

VOL. VIII, No. II. MAY, 1895.

METROPOLITAN PAMPHLET SERIES.

ISSUED QUARTERLY:

Subscription Price, 2s. or 50 Cents.   Price per Copy, 6d. or 15 Cents.

SMOCKING,

FANCY STITCHES

AND

CROSS-STITCH AND DARNED-NET DESIGNS.

PUBLISHED BY

THE BUTTERICK PUBLISHING CO.

(LIMITED),

LONDON AND NEW YORK.

SMOCKING,

FANCY STITCHES,

AND

CROSS-STITCH AND DARNED-NET

DESIGNS.

Smocking, Fancy Stitches,

AND

CROSS-STITCH AND DARNED-NET DESIGNS.

DIRECTIONS FOR MAKING SMOCKING OR HONEY-COMBING.

The recent revival of smocking or honey-combing has resulted in a number of pretty arrangements of this decorative work and also in the adaptation of numerous fancy stitches, which increase its ornamental effect and give much variety in the way of design.

Of the two methods of making the smocking or honey-combing—the American and the

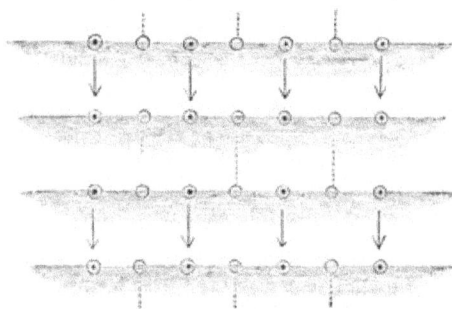

Figure No. 1.

English—the former is rather the simpler, but the result is exactly the same in each instance, and in both the elasticity of the work is equal. The two methods are clearly described in this article, and the illustrations are very plain; either method may be followed according to taste, and both are here adopted for the diamond pattern, which is the easiest and most popular, and to which great variety may be given by fancy stitches. Another style of smocking or honey-combing which is very different in effect and permits some beautiful arrangements of designs and stitches is also illustrated and described, and it will be much used on account of its elaborate effect.

The honey-combing is very effectively displayed in yokes and in the upper part of tennis and other blouses, in tea-gowns, ladies', misses' and children's dresses, and in matinées, breakfast jackets, school gowns, etc.; it may also take the shape of a

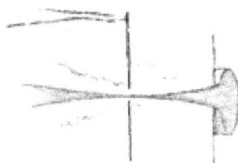

Figure No. 2.
FIGURES NOS. 1 AND 2.—AMERICAN METHOD OF SMOCKING.
(For Descriptions of Figures Nos. 1 and 2, see " American Method of Smocking.")

Swiss girdle, a straight or curved belt or a corselet. Sleeves of smocked gowns are honey-combed at the wrists or near the shoulders, and hat crowns of cloth and suiting are elaborated in an effective way by this decoration.

In order to do the smocking well great care should be taken to space evenly. Two methods of spacing which may be followed for either style are illustrated and described. Soft, loosely-twisted embroidery silk for smocking woollens and silks, and the best quality of French embroidery cotton for washable goods are the best for this purpose, and a double thread should never be employed. Two or three over-and-over stitches suffice to hold the folds, and the thread should not be broken. The silk or cotton may be of the same color as the material or of a contrasting color, and frequently two or three colors are introduced to give a brilliant effect. Beads often lend their brilliancy to sober garments, and they may match or differ from the goods in color but should not be large. Under the honey-combing a smooth section of lining is

Figure No. 3.

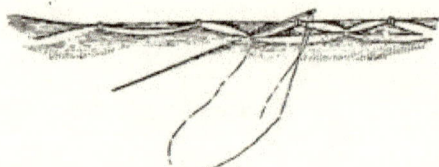

Figure No. 4.

needed to prevent it from stretching, and between this lining and the smocking a piece of crinoline shaped like the lining is usually placed to give firmness. Only the outer edges of the lining need be caught to the smocking.

The simplest and most effective fancy stitches for decorating smocking are also illustrated and described in this article, and their effect on smooth parts is displayed.

Figure No. 5.

Figures Nos. 3, 4 and 5.—American Method of Smocking.
(For Descriptions of Figures Nos. 3, 4 and 5, see "American Method of Smocking.")

The American method of honey-combing we have published for several months, but will republish it here for the accomodation of our patrons and for comparison with the English method.

The diamond design is the one adapted to all our patterns for smocked garments.

American Method of Smocking.

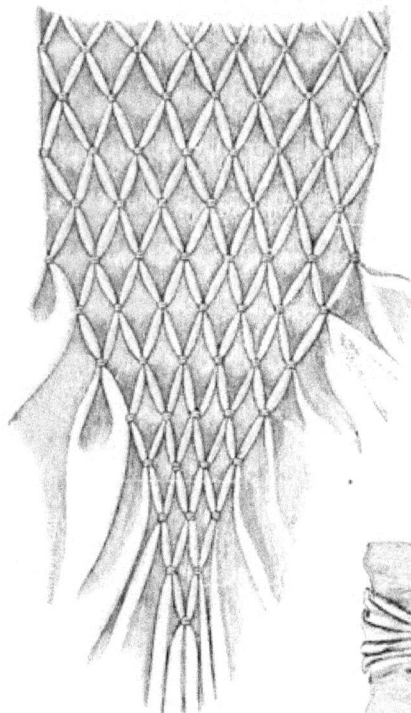

FIGURES Nos. 1, 2, 3, 4, 5, 6 and 7 — AMERICAN METHOD OF SMOCKING OR HONEY-COMBING. — The smocking perfected is shown at figure No. 6, which also illustrates how it may be run to a point when desired. The first thing to do is to space evenly, and this is shown at figure No. 1. The section to be smocked may be creased or marked off in lines with thread or chalk in the direction the smocking is to run, and then on each line dots are made to indicate where the catching together is done. If preferred, the spaces may be marked by using cardboard as described below in the English method. This marking method will do for all but sheer and delicate-hued fabrics when marked

FIGURE No. 6.

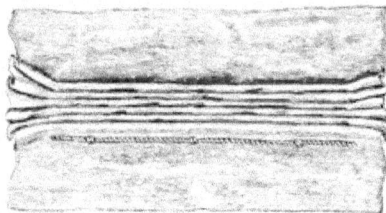

FIGURE No. 7.

FIGURES Nos. 6 AND 7.—AMERICAN METHOD OF SMOCKING.
(For Descriptions of Figures Nos. 6 and 7, see "American Method of Smocking.")

SMOCKING, FANCY STITCHES,

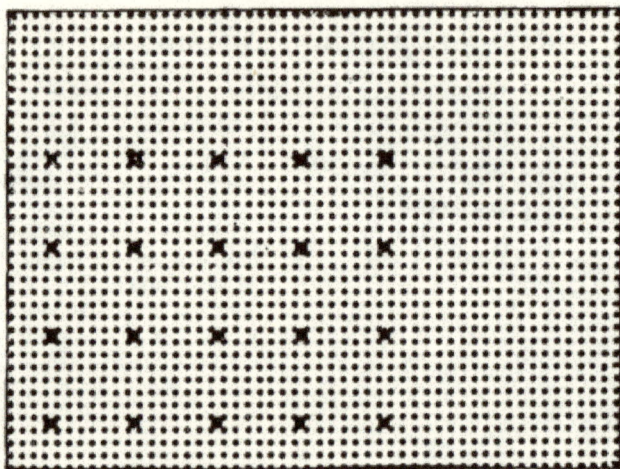

FIGURE No. 8.

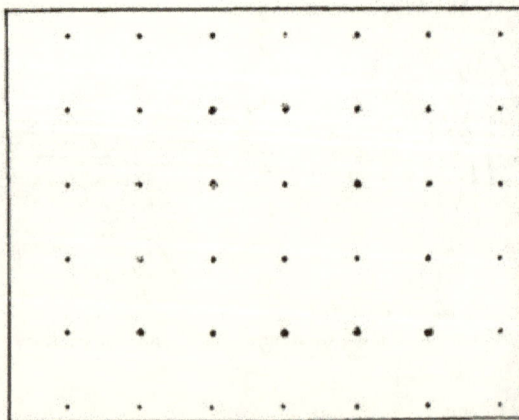

FIGURE No. 9.

FIGURES NOS. 8 AND 9.—ENGLISH METHOD OF SMOCKING.
(For Descriptions of Figures Nos. 8 and 9 see "English Method of Smocking.")

paper will have to be fully examine figure No. the arrows are to be instance, and those con- lines are to be similarly most space; catch together arrows, beginning at the right; insert the needle as shown at figure No. 2, and make the fastening securely, two or three over-and-over stitches being usually sufficient; then pass the needle under- neath and out through the as illustrated at figure No. uer described to the end

Now begin at the sec- gether the dots connected ing the needle underneath dot just below, as shown the needle through as il- and make the tacking se- row is done in the same ed the work will not be thread should lie between side is illustrated at figure

used as in tucking. Care- 1; the dots indicated by caught together in every nected by the dotted caught. Begin at the top- the dots indicated by the next arrow dot below, 3. Continue in the man- of the line.

ond space and catch to- by the broken lines, pass- and out through the lined at figure No. 4; then pass lustrated at figure No. 5 cure. Each succeeding way. Once properly start- tedious. The way the the folds on the wrong No. 7.

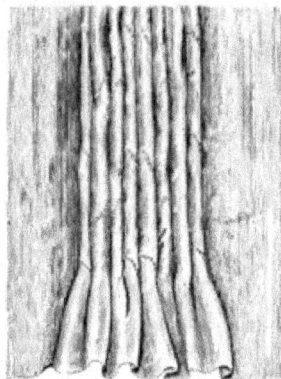

FIGURE No. 11.

FIGURES Nos. 10 AND 11.—ENGLISH METHOD OF SMOCKING.—(For Description of Figures Nos. 10 and 11, see "English Method of Smocking.")

English Method of Smocking or Honey-Combing.

FIGURES NOS. 8, 9, 10 AND 11.—ENGLISH METHOD OF SMOCKING OR HONEY-COMBING. — The use of perforated cardboard in marking the spaces for smocking or honey-combing is here illustrated. Take a piece of perforated cardboard of convenient size—a piece about three times as long and three times as wide as figure No. 8 is a good size—; cut out with a penknife a number of small holes at equal intervals, leaving five perforations between each hole, as shown by figure No. 8. The cutting will be most easily done by laying the cardboard on a piece of wood or on a table. Then lay the cardboard on the goods and mark dots on the goods through the holes, either with a pencil or with a finely pointed piece of chalk, as shown at figure No. 9. The marking should be all done before the smocking is commenced, as it is not easy to do it afterward. When all the holes in the

FIGURE NO. 12.

card are marked by dots on the goods the card is moved along or down, as required, with one row of holes over the last row of dots made. The dots are caught together as explained in the American method, with this difference — the thread is brought diagonally underneath, as shown at figure No. 10, instead of straight up and down as in the method above described. Care should be taken not to draw the threads too tightly. When the work is properly done the back of the smocking will appear as at figure No. 11. The smocking is done in lines from top to bottom, one line being finished before another is commenced; and the thread should always be kept to the right of the needle. Two or three over-and-over stitches will suffice to make the fastening, and care should be taken not to entangle the threads in the folds on the wrong side.

FIGURE NO. 13

FIGURES NOS. 12 AND 13.—FANCY STITCHING FOR DIAMOND SMOCKING.

(For Descriptions of Figures Nos. 12 and 13, see "Fancy Stitching for Diamond Smocking.")

FANCY STITCHING FOR DIAMOND SMOCKING.

FIGURES NOS. 12 AND 13.—FANCY STITCHING FOR DECORATING DIAMOND SMOCKING OR HONEY-COMBING.— Embroidery silk or floss of any preferred shade may be used for these stitches. Pass the needle from underneath, bringing it through just under a tacking; then carry the thread over the tacking, pass the needle under the tacking from the top and out through the fold at the left end of the tacking; then carry it across, inserting the needle at the left end of the tacking and drawing it out through the right fold just below the tacking, as shown by figures Nos. 12 and 13. Figure No. 12 shows the first two insertions of the needle, and figure No. 13 the last or finishing stitch. The stitching is done in diagonal rows that run in two directions.

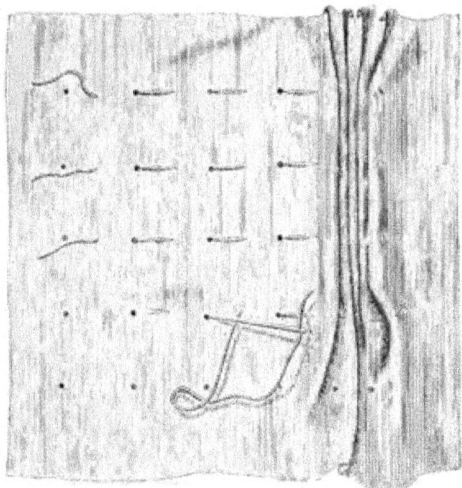

FIGURE NO. 14.—METHOD OF GATHERING MATERIAL FOR FANCY SMOCKING OR HONEY-COMBING.

(For Description see "Fancy Smocking.")

FANCY SMOCKING.

FIGURE NO. 14.—METHOD OF GATHERING MATERIAL FOR FANCY SMOCKING OR HONEY-COMBING.— For this gathering the material is marked as described for the diamond smocking and is then gathered up with long stitches, the needle being passed in at one dot and out midway between this dot and the next, as shown at figure No. 14; the gatherings are done in lines, and each thread is drawn up closely and fastened over a pin and each fold creased lengthwise over the fingers with the needle as in gauging. When this is done the work is ready for any ornamental arrangement of stitching, some of the most beautiful designs being shown at figures Nos. 15, 16, 17, 18 and 19, described on the next page.

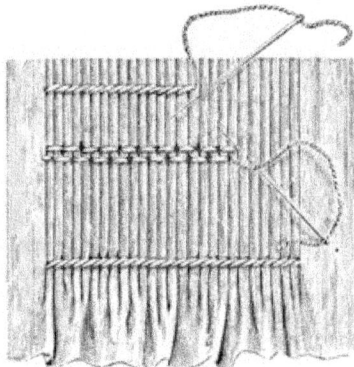

FIGURE NO. 15.—ORNAMENTAL ROPE-STITCHING FOR FANCY SMOCKING.

(For Description of Figure No. 15 see "Ornamental Stitching for Fancy Smocking.")

ORNAMENTAL STITCHING FOR FANCY SMOCKING.

FIGURES NOS. 15, 16, 17, 18 AND 19.—ORNAMENTAL ROPE-STITCHING FOR FANCY SMOCKING OR HONEY-COMBING.—The rope stitch is illustrated at figure No. 15, and is neither more nor less than the well-known outline or back-stitch; the needle is passed through each fold from underneath to the outside, and the work is done from left to right as illustrated. The same stitch is used in making the middle row of stitching in figure No. 15, but each alternate stitch is made above the one below as pictured, producing what are called separated rope - stitches. Care should be taken to make these separated stitches evenly, else the effect will not be satisfactory.

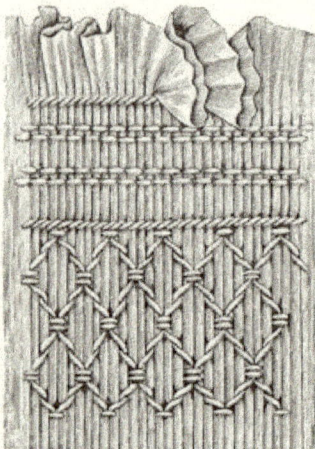

FIGURE No. 16.

FIGURE No. 17.

These two arrangements of the rope-stitch are shown in a pretty design at figure No. 16. The solid rope stitching heads a frill, and above it are two rows of the separated stitches, a little above which is a row of solid rope-stitching which comes at the foot of a diamond design done in the separated stitches. This design may be made uniform by marking the gathered portion by means of the cardboard and pencil. In arranging this smocking for the yoke of a dress wrapper, etc., the ruffle may be placed at the neck, carefully hemmed or faced and tacked to form a shell ruching, which may lie upon a pretty ruff of lace, crêpe lisse, etc.

The separated rope-stitch is used at figure No. 17; there are two lines of separated stitches above a frill and above these a double lattice design is done with separated stitches accurately spaced.

Figure No. 18 illustrates two rows of the diamond smocking with a row of the fancy smocking between. This is done by making one row of the diamond smocking as deep as desired and gathering it up at both ends as described for the fancy smocking. Three similar rows of gatherings are made till the depth desired for the fancy smock-

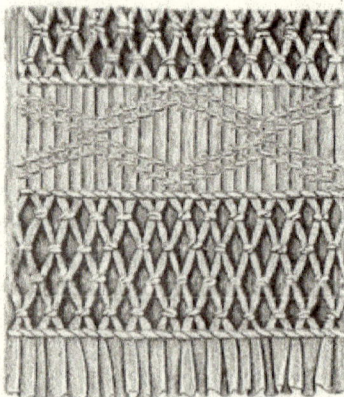

FIGURE No. 18.

FIGURES NOS. 16. 17 AND 18.—ORNAMENTAL ROPE-STITCHING FOR FANCY SMOCKING.

(For Descriptions of Figures Nos. 16, 17 and 18, see "Ornamental Stitching for Fancy Smocking.")

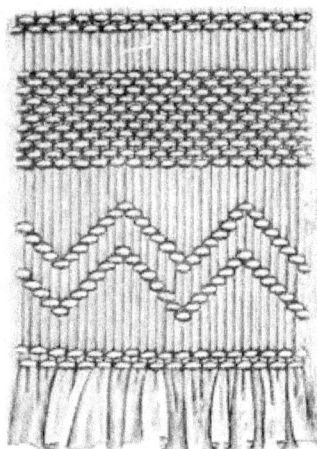

FIGURE NO. 19.

FIGURE No. 19.—ORNAMENTAL ROPE-STITCHING FOR
FANCY SMOCKING.

For description of Figure No. 19 see "Ornamental
Stitching for Fancy Smocking."

ing is obtained, and then the diamond smocking is again begun and contiued to the required depth. The two styles of smocking are defined by rows of rope-stitching; and in the fancy smocking is made a Virginia-fence design, the stitches being very evenly arranged in the outline or rope-stitch which is plainly described at figure No. 15 on page 9.

At figure No. 19 the solid and separated rope-stitches are combined in a simple but elaborate-looking design; there are two rows of separated stitches above a frill, which may be hemmed or faced; then a double lattice design of solid rope-stitches, then a broad band design of the separated stitches, and above this two rows of separated stitches. Of course, the smocking may be continued to the edge, so as to do away with the frill, but the frill makes a pretty neck or wrist finish.

All of the designs in fancy stitching upon the following pages are as appropriate for the same garments as the diamond smocking. The work should be held so that the folds will run up and down instead of across the fingers. If the eye is not a sufficient guide for the design, the perforated card-board should be used, and the design outlined with thread or a pencil or piece of chalk. Long stitches of contrasting cotton are really the best to use in planning out these designs, as they leave no mark in the goods and are easily drawn out, after the embroidery stitches are put in.

DIAMOND SMOCKING FOR INFANTS' GARMENTS.

Diamond smocking is quite extensively used for the yokes and sleeves of infants' garments, not only because it is ornamental but on account of its elasticity. The advantage of the latter quality will be readily appreciated, as every one knows how quickly growing babies and children get beyond the limits of the unyielding portions of their little garments, thus soon rendering the latter useless.

Among the daintiest of these smocked garments for babies are little wrappers or house robes of India silk. They are composed of two or three breadths of the material joined along the selvedges. The breadths are smocked in round-yoke style at the top and hemmed by feather-stitching at the bottom. The material is doubled over at the top before the smocking is begun, in order to form a frill about the neck. The sleeves are full at the top, and are turned under at the bottom for a frill and completed with a band formed by smocking the fabric above the frill. This is but one garment of many similar ones; but its description will afford ideas and suggestions to both the actual and the expectant mother, which will no doubt result in pretty as well as sensible additions to the wardrobe of the young sovereign of the household or that of the little stranger whose coming is awaited.

In decorating these dainty little garments with smocking and fancy stitches, white silk may be used upon white fabrics, or upon tinted materials such as silk or cashmere in pale-pink, pale-blue, yellow or lavender. Or, any of these tints in the embroidery thread may be used upon white. Pale-blue or pale-pink is especially pretty upon white when used to make the smocking, as it marks the diamonds of the latter by tiny bead-like dots that are very soft and effective in appearance. When tinted silk is used for the smocking, it is also used for the fancy stitching along hems and edges. A little coat or cloak of white silk or cashmere, smocked with pale-pink silk and lined with Surah silk of the same shade would make a charmingly dainty garment for a young infant.

ORNAMENTAL TACKS AND EMBROIDERED ORNAMENTS

FOR TAILOR-MADE AND OTHER GARMENTS.

One of the attractions of a tailor-made garment is its generally exquisite finish. The latter consists in the manner in which the linings are inserted, the exactness with which edges are finished, the perfect pressing of the seams and, finally, the ornamental tacks and embroidered ornaments with which corners and seam-ends are completed.

It is the impression among many dressmakers that no one but a tailor can successfully add the latter finish to a garment; but if even an ordinarily intelligent seamstress will follow the directions and illustrations here given, she will find that with a little practice she will be able to as nicely complete a garment with ornamental tackings, etc., as can a tailor; and this accomplishment will render her services of greater value to her employers from the more perfectly finished work she will be able to do.

The simplest staying tack, known as the bar-tack, is shown partly made at figure No. 1. It is much used at the ends of pocket openings, etc. The detail of this tack is as follows: First decide on the length of the tack, marking the line with chalk; then pass the needle up from underneath at one end of the line, down through at the opposite point, up again at the starting point, and down again at the opposite end; and make as many of these long stitches as desired. Not less than two stitches should be made, but as many more may be made as the worker may elect—the greater the number, the thicker and heavier will be the tack. Then, without breaking the thread, bring the needle up at one end, just to one side of the upper and under long stitches, and pass it down at a point exactly opposite on the other side of the long stitches, to form a short stitch that will be square across the long stitches on top. Cover the entire length of the long stitches with such short stitches, being careful to bring the needle up at the same side of the long stitches every time, so that the *under* part of the long stitches will be crossed as well as the *upper* part, and pressing the long stitches together with the needle so as to produce as narrow and high an effect as possible.

In garments that are finished with machine-stitching, bar-tacks at the ends of pocket openings usually extend from a second row of stitching above the opening to a second row below the opening, and are sometimes crossed at the ends with short bar-tacks, as illustrated at figure No. 2.

Tacks that are commonly called arrow-heads are seen in a variety of shapes and stitches, and are made at the tops of plaits and laps and at the ends of seams and pocket openings. One of the simplest of these tacks is illustrated in detail at figure No. 3, and completed at figure No. 4. To make this style of tack, mark an outline of the tack with chalk or a pencil. Bring the needle up through at point A and pass it down at point B; then up inside and very close to point B, and down on the center line close to point A; up at point A, exactly where the needle was first passed through and down at point C; up inside and close to point C, and down on the center line exactly at the second stitch extending from B to A. Fill in the entire outline in this way, always making two stitches on one side and then two on the other, and being careful to keep all the stitches even on the center line. At figure No. 3 the work is shown with three stitches on one side and two on the other, and the needle correctly placed for the fourth stitch on line B A.

A more artistic and durable arrow-head is depicted completed at figure No. 10, and in detail at figures Nos. 5, 6, 7, 8 and 9. Mark the outline with chalk or a pencil. Bring the needle up at point A, and pass it down at point B; then up inside and very close to point B, down on the line AC close to point A, and up at point A outside and very close to the first stitch made. Then pass the needle under the second stitch and down at point C, as illustrated at figure No. 5. Bring the needle up inside and close to point C and then pass it down near point A outside and very close to the first stitch made, as shown at figure No. 6. Next bring the needle up outside and very close to the first stitch running from A to C, and quite close to the second stitch in line AB; and then pass it down near B, as illustrated at figure No. 7. Bring the needle up again on line BC inside and close to the third stitch in line AB; and pass it down outside the first stitch on line AC, as represented at figure No. 8. Then bring the needle up outside and very close to the first stitch on the line AB, pass it under the fourth stitch in line AB and down on line CB, close to the second stitch on line AC, as illustrated at figure No. 9. Now bring the needle up on line CB close to the third stitch on line AC, and pass it down outside the first stitch on line AB close to the third stitch on line AC. Proceed in this manner to fill in the outline, always making two stitches parallel with line AB, then

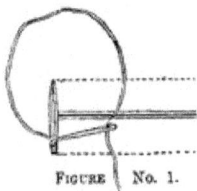

FIGURE No. 1.

FIGURE No. 2.

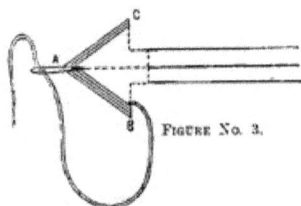

FIGURE No. 3.

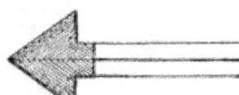

FIGURE No. 4.

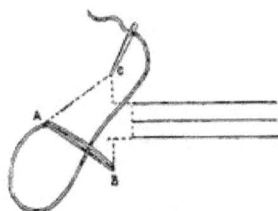

FIGURE No. 5.

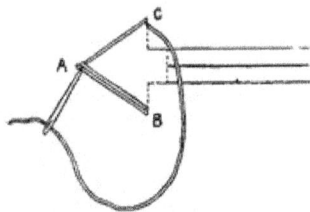

FIGURE No. 6.

two stitches parallel with line AC, and being careful to pass the third, fifth, seventh, etc., stitches, running parallel with line AC, respectively under the second, fourth, sixth, eighth, etc., stitches running parallel with line AB, as illustrated at figures Nos. 5 and 9.

Other fanciful arrow-heads are displayed at figures Nos. 11 and 12. They are worked exactly as described for that shown at figure No. 10.

The diamond ornament represented at figure No. 13 is made by working close together two arrow-heads like that shown at figure No. 12.

Every point of the star ornament portrayed at figure No. 15 is filled in exactly as described for working the arrow-head illustrated at figure No. 10. One point should be completely filled in at a

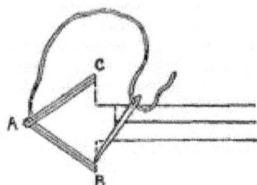

time. The correct outline for a five-pointed star is given at figure No. 14, and the size displayed at this figure will prove effective for decorative purposes. The star may be copied on tracing-paper and the tracing used as a pattern; or, if a larger or smaller star be desired, a circle may be drawn, as indicated by the dotted line, and divded into five equal parts, and the points may then be carefully formed. One point in the outline is shown completely filled in, while another shows the detail of the work as described at figure No. 9.

FIGURE No. 7.

Probably the most ornamental of the fancy tacks ordinarily used at the ends of pocket openings and seams is the crow-tack. It is illustrated completely at figure

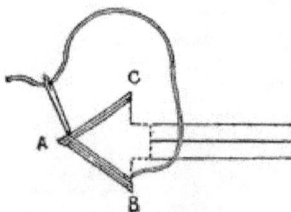

FIGURE No. 8.

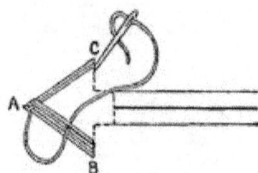

FIGURE No. 9.

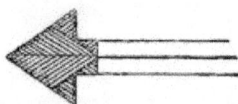

FIGURE No. 10.

FIGURE No. 11.

No. 18, and in detail at figures Nos. 16 and 17. Outline the tack with chalk or a pencil. The dotted outline seen at figure No. 16 shows the correct outline for the tack. Bring the needle up at point A, and pass it down at B, and up again at B outside and close to the stitch in line AB, then down at C, up at C outside and close to the stitch in line BC, and down at A just outside the stitch in line AB as illustrated at figure No. 16. Now bring the needle up on dotted line AC outside the stitch on line AC close to A; and pass it down on dotted line BC outside the stitch on line BC close to B; up on dotted line AB outside both stitches on line AB close to B; down on dotted line CA outside the stitch on line CA close to C; up on dotted line BC outside both stitches on line BC

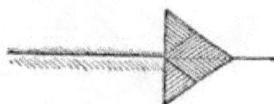

FIGURE No. 12.

FIGURE No. 13.

and down on dotted line AB outside both stitches on line AB, as illustrated at figure No. 17. Fill in the entire outline in this way, until the completed tack looks like figure No. 18. It will be noticed in making this tack that all the stitches are taken on the dotted lines and always outside the made stitches, thus compressing the stitches so as to curve the sides of the tack.

A basket pattern in square and diamond shapes is produced on the ornaments shown at figures Nos. 21 and 22. The diamond or square should be outlined in the size required with chalk or a pencil, and the sides should be marked off evenly into three, five, seven or more spaces, according to the size of the basket pattern desired—the greater the number of spaces the smaller the basket pattern will be when worked.

The work is illustrated in detail at figures Nos. 19 and 20. Outline a square and mark off

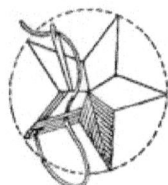

FIGURE No. 14.

FIGURE No. 15.

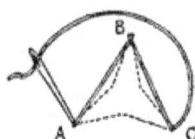

FIGURE No. 16.

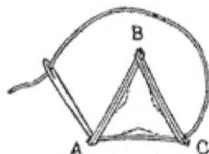

FIGURE No. 17.

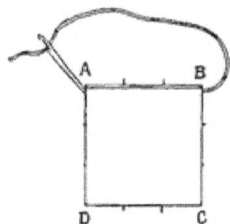

FIGURE No. 18.

each side into three equal spaces. Bring the needle up at corner A, and pass it down at B up close to B on line BC, and down close to A on line AD, as illustrated at figure No. 19. Fill in the square in this way, being careful to make the same number of stitches in each marked-off space, and enough stitches to thoroughly cover the goods. In this instance twenty-seven stitches were used to fill in the square—nine in each space.

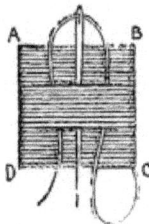

FIGURE No. 19.

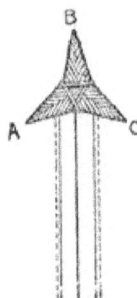

FIGURE No. 20.

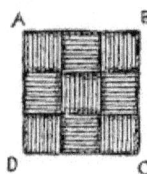

FIGURE No. 21.

FIGURE No. 22.

To make the basket pattern: Bring the needle up at corner C outside and close to the last stitch in line DC; pass it, (eye first so as not to split the thread,) under the nine stitches in the middle space as illustrated at figure No. 20; and then pass it down at corner B outside and close to the first stitch on line AB. Now bring the needle up close to this stitch on line AB, and pass it under the same nine stitches in the same way, and down near the corner C. Continue in this way until nine stitches are made in this space. Now make nine stitches in the next space, passing the needle *under* the first group of nine, *over* the second group of nine and *under* the remaining group of nine. The last group of nine stitches is made exactly as directed for the first group. Any number of spaces may be filled in this way, the needle being passed alternately under and over the groups of stitches in the spaces.

The diamond ornament illustrated at figure No. 22 is worked exactly like the square, and so is every variety of ornament in even basket pattern.

The anchor is a very graceful ornament for sailor suits, etc.; and when correctly outlined, it requires very little labor to produce a good effect. It may be of any size to suit the location for which it is intended. Three useful sizes are illustrated at figures Nos. 23, 24 and 25. Mark the outline with chalk or a pencil; then fill in the outline with long stitches, catching them to the material wherever necessary to keep them within the outline, and making a sufficient number of stitches to form a padding thick enough to produce a high rolled effect when the embroidery stitches are worked in. Work the points of the anchor exactly as directed for fancy arrow-heads, the detail of which is illustrated and described at figures Nos. 5, 6, 7, 8 and 9.

FIGURE No. 23.

FIGURE No. 24.

Work in the embroidery stitches, passing the needle in at one side of the outline and out at the opposite side, making the stitches in over-and-over style and very close together, and being careful to take the stitches evenly on the outline and to draw them to an equal tension. The anchor may be outlined to slant to the right or to the left, as required, and may be traced on tracing paper, and the tracing cut out for a pattern that can be placed as desired.

These tacks and ornaments are generally worked with coarse button-hole twist.

FIGURE No. 25.

Designs for Corners, Pockets, Cuffs, Collars, Laps or Other Sections of Garments

A passing glance at the the designs under the above heading will disclose to the observer and the needle-woman their adaptability to the purposes mentioned, and the simplicity of their formations. No explanation of details is needed. Like other designs upon following pages, they may be enlarged or reduced to any size desired, the latter depending entirely on the space to be decorated.

FIGURE No. 1.

FIGURE No. 2.

FIGURE No. 3.

FIGURE No. 4.

In selecting the thread to be used in developing these designs, care should be exercised in making the selections harmonious as to color, and appropriate as to the texture of the fabric to be decorated. Brown upon écru, a deep gray upon a pearl or light gray ground, or dense red on wood tints are pretty combinations

2

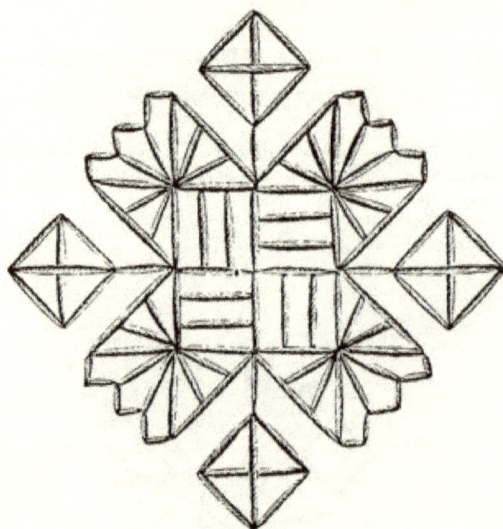

FIGURE No. 5.

FIGURE No. 6.

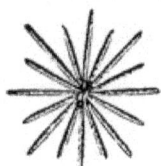

FIGURE No. 7.

FIGURE No. 8

FIGURE No. 9.

    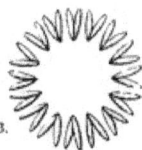

FIGURE No. 11.   FIG. No. 12.   FIGURE No. 13.

FIGURE No. 10.

FIGURE No. 14

FIGURE No. 15.   FIGURE No. 16.   FIGURE No. 17.

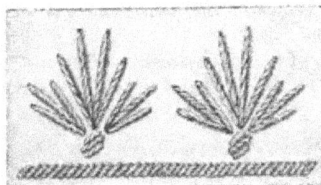

FIGURE No. 18.

Fancy Stitches for the Decoration of Garments.

HONEY-COMB, BRICK AND DIAMOND STITCHES.

The group of stitches given below presents several new varieties in this class of decoration. Any one of the designs may be applied as a border to a skirt, apron, cloak, or any garment further decorated by smocking; or it may be used alone upon any garment for which it seems appropriate. White or colored silk or working cotton or linen is generally selected for making fancy stitches upon garments.

FIGURES NOS. 1, 2 AND 3.—HONEY-COMB STITCHES.—These stitches are all made upon the

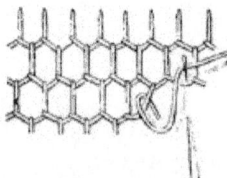

FIGURE No. 1.

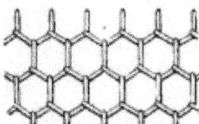

FIGURE No. 2.

FIGURE No. 3.

FIGURES NOS. 1, 2 AND 3.—HONEY-COMB STITCHES.

FIGURE No. 4.—DIAMOND-STITCH.

same principle, and the latter is fully shown at figure No. 1. The method is as follows for the work seen at this engraving: Make a row of button-hole stitches along the portion of the garment to be decorated. Then make the second and every following row in the same manner, except that the stitches are taken through those of the first row, and the latter stitches are slightly pulled down as seen in the engraving, to produce the

honey-comb outlines. The engraving shows just how the needle is set for every stitch.

FIGURE No. 4.—DIAMOND-STITCH.—This is a very pretty finish and, as will be observed by an inspection of the engraving, one easily made. The diamond crossings are first made and then secured by back-stitches set as shown in the picture. This stitch is sometimes called Imitation Smocking.

FIGURE No. 5.—BRICK-STITCH.—This stitch is made by first applying long parallel lines of the working cotton or silk. Then bar these threads off into brick outlines by the method shown in the picture. This will fasten each horizontal line in place and produce a neat effect.

FIGURE No. 5.—BRICK STITCH.

FIGURE No. 6.—BAR-STITCH.

FIGURE No. 6.—BAR-STITCH.—First make a series of quite long, horizontal stitches, set as shown in the engraving, and then cross them diagonally by a sort of over-and-over stitch taken so as to bring the working cotton over the ends of the horizontal stitches. The engraving renders the work perfectly easy to do, as it clearly represents the result desired.

PLAIN AND FANCY HERRING-BONE, FEATHER, BRIAR AND OTHER DECORATIVE STITCHES.

The stitches illustrated below represent the principle of almost all of the fancy stitches used in the decoration of garments by such methods. They are used for hems, bands, belts and any edge along which they are suitable as a finish. Ordinary embroidery silk is generally used in making them when the garment is of silk or wool. For garments of wash fabrics, wash embroidery-silk, or cotton or linen floss is used.

FIGURE No. 1.—This engraving shows a stitch called indiscriminately by two names—cat-stitch and herring-bone. The picture shows just how the work progresses from *left* to *right*. The needle is set for a stitch in the *upper row*, and when it is made, the needle is set again for a similar stitch in the *lower row*. Figure No. 3 shows how it is used for hemming, the hem being turned over on the outside of the garment. This is also a method much used in hemming draperies of heavy fabrics, the hem being widely turned on the under side in the ordinary manner, but not at the raw edge of the goods. The latter edge is held down smoothly and securely by the stitching described, and thus no ridge or line shows through on the outside.

FIGURE No. 2.—This engraving represents plain feather-stitching, sometimes also called briar-stitching. The method of making is clearly illustrated and the application of the stitch to the edge of a hem is also shown by figure No. 4.

Another variety of fancy stitch is shown at figures Nos. 7 and 13 on page 22; and all of

FIGURE No. 1.

FIGURE No. 2.

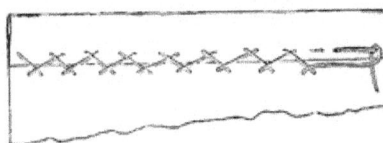

FIGURE No. 3.

the stitches seen upon pages 21, 22, 23 and 24, except figure No. 32, are formed upon the foundation-principles of the ones on this page and that of figures Nos. 7 and 13. As the latter methods are also clearly delineated by the pictures, no difficulty will be experienced in reproducing any of the stitches illustrated.

Dainty shades of lavender, pink, blue and green, bright tints of yellow, red, brown and blue, and soft heliotrope, old-rose, gobelin and tan colors are all employed for decorating garments with fancy stitches, when white is not particularly or definitely desired.

FIGURE No. 4.

The group of stitches shown below are appropriate for the decoration of gowns, dresses, wrappers, coats, cloaks. aprons, petticoats, or any garment for an adult or a child which requires a dainty

FIGURE No. 5.

FIGURE No. 6.

FIGURE No. 7.

FIGURE No. 8.

FIGURE No. 9.

FIGURE No. 10.

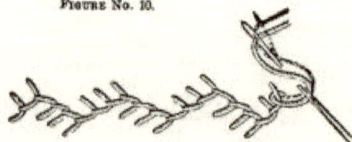

FIGURE No. 11.

FIGURE No. 12.

FIGURE No. 13.

FIGURE No. 14.

FIGURE No. 15.

finish in connection with smocking or honey-combing; or, either variety may be used by itself or above frills of lace or plaitings of the material, or as a heading to ruffles of pinked silk.

The engravings upon this page show a number of fancy stitches which have for their foundation-principles those of the first two stitches shown upon page 21. Figure No. 16 shows another method of securing a hem by fancy stitches, as does figure No. 20; and one detail of figure No. 16 may

FIGURE No. 16.

FIGURE No. 17.

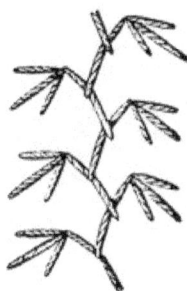

FIGURE No. 18.

FIGURE No. 19.

FIGURE No. 20.

FIGURE No. 21.

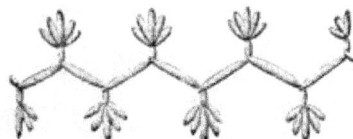

FIGURE No. 22.

FIGURE No. 23.

also be seen by referring to figure No. 5 on page 22; while figure No. 13 on page 22 also shows the detail of figure No. 20. Figures Nos. 18 and 21 are pretty designs for babies' blankets, petticoats and little house sacks. When tinted material is selected, use white silk for the fancy stitches.

The fancy stitches here seen require no description as to detail or application. The design seen at No. 28 may be enlarged or diminished to any size desired, according to the requirements

FIGURE No. 24.

FIGURE No. 25.

FIGURE No. 26.

FIGURE No. 27.

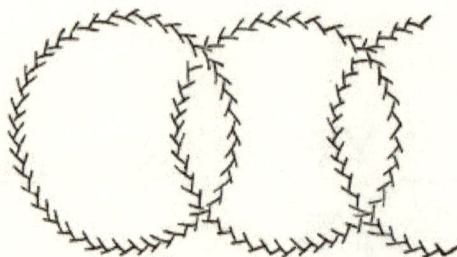

FIGURE No. 28.—DESIGN IN HERRING-BONE STITCH.

FIGURE No. 29.

FIGURE No. 30.

of the garment to be decorated. The size given in the engraving mentioned is suitable for children's garments, and may be done in white or colored silks.

FIGURE No. 32.—ROPE-STITCH.—This stitch is made as follows: Bring the needle up from the back of the work and pick up a little of the fabric, bringing the needle out a little above the point where the working thread is brought through from the

FIGURE No. 31.

FIGURE No. 32.

back. The engraving shows just how the work is done and where the thread lies after the above detail is worked out. Repeat this stitch to form all of the outline desired.

FIGURE No. 33.

FIGURE No. 34.

FIGURE No. 35.

FIGURE No. 36.

FIGURE No. 37.

FIGURE No. 40.

FIGURE No. 41.

FIGURE No. 42.

FIG. No. 38. FIG. No. 39.

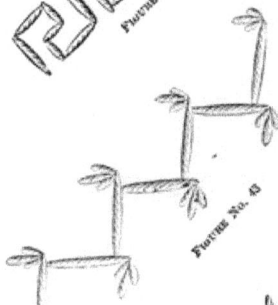

FIGURE No. 43.

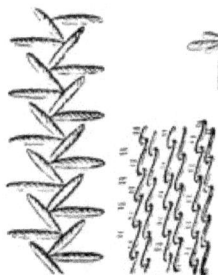

FIGURE No. 46.

FIGURE No. 44. FIGURE No. 45.

FIG. No. 47. FIG. No. 48.

FIGURE No. 49

FIGURE No. 50.

FANCY KNOT AND COMBINATION STITCHES.

Knot-stitches form pretty variations when used in combination with other stitches. The engraving at figure No. 1 represents the covered knot-stitch, made by taking an ordinary back-

FIGURE No. 1.

FIGURE No. 2.

FIGURE No. 3.

FIGURE No. 4.

FIGURE No. 5.

FIGURE No. 6.

FIGURE No. 7.

FIGURE No. 8.

FIGURE No. 9.

FIGURE No. 10.

FIGURE No. 11.

FIGURE No. 12.

stitch, winding the floss twice about the needle and then drawing the latter through, with the left thumb held closely over the coil. The needle point is then thrust to the other side almost exactly where it came to the surface, so as to locate another knot. This stitch is frequently adopted in making initials, handkerchief-corners or any fine embroidery of that variety.

FIGURE No. 3 shows the wound knot-stitch which is used for the same purposes as the covered knot-stitch described, and is made as follows: The needle is set, wound and drawn

FIGURE No. 13.

FIGURE No. 14.

through, the same as in the first stitch, and is then thrust through the outside at the place indicated by the dot seen above the needle at figure No. 1. This draws the wound thread into the knot illustrated, which is just as pretty as its predecessor. This style of stitch appears in all fine French work.

A knotted outline stitch is shown at figure No. 2 where the detail of its formation is perfectly illustrated. The remaining engravings under this heading represent a number of very pretty combinations easy to follow and effective in result.

BARB, BATTLEMENT, BLANKET AND PALING STITCHES.

FIGURES Nos. 1 AND 2.—BARB-STITCH. —These figures show the barb-stitch, used for decorating garments of all kinds. The first part of the stitch is the ordinary button-hole stitch made coarsely. Figure No. 2 clearly depicts the position of the needle in both lines, showing how the stitch is accomplished. Two rows of button-hole stitching are placed back to back as shown at figure No. 1. The stitches must be made very evenly, or the effect will not be good; and the barbs are made to come in between those of the opposite row. For the second part of the stitch, bring the needle up in the corner of the angle in the lower row, and put it down at the corner of the angle in the upper row, and so on, making a succession of overcasting stitches like this all the way across the line. The stitch may be developed in all kinds of crewel, worsted, silk or cotton, and colors may be used to suit the taste.

FIGURE No. 1.

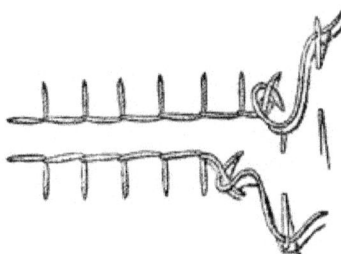

FIGURE No. 2.

FIGURES Nos. 1 AND 2.—BARB-STITCH.

FIGURE No. 3.—BATTLEMENT-STITCH.—This is an uncommon and novel stitch, and is very effective for bordering large scroll designs, laying down hems, etc. It looks best when worked in four shades of the same color, but two contrasting colors will also be pretty. First work a row of button-hole stitches in the lightest shade, making the stitches half an inch in length and half an inch

FIGURE No. 3.—BATTLEMENT-STITCH.

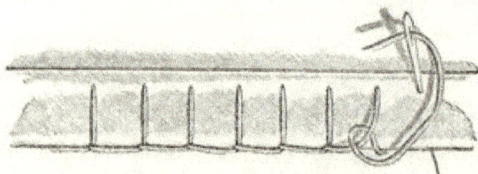

FIGURE No. 4.—BLANKET-STITCH.

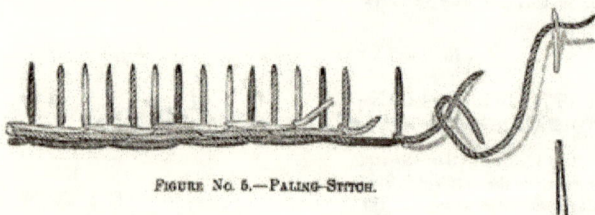

FIGURE No. 5.—PALING-STITCH.

apart. This first row should be very evenly made, slanting the stitches as illustrated, for upon its
evenness depends the regularity of the following rows, and, consequently, the effect of the completed
work. When the first row is finished, commence at the left-hand side, and work a second row of
button-holing on the top of the first, but a little to the left of and a little below it. Then work a third
row a little to the left of and a little below the second row. Work a fourth row in the same manner,
using the silks in order, from the lightest to the darkest shades. In the last row the tops of the
stitches should come a little above the horizontal threads of the first row. The stitch is very decorative
for baby-afghans, small stand-covers, aprons, fancy scarfs, etc., and will be effective on the yokes of
infants' and children's dresses when worked in white or colored Madonna cotton, or linen thread.

FIGURE No. 4.—BLANKET-STITCH.—This stitch is represented as being made on the edge of a
hem as it is only adaptable to such applications. To make the stitch: Put the needle through the
opening at the end of the hem, bringing it out at the edge; now pass it through the hem about
half an inch to the right and the same distance above the edge, drawing it down to the edge of the
hem, and throwing the loop over the needle; this forms a button-hole stitch, as illustrated.

FIGURE No. 5.—PALING-STITCH.—This novel and pretty stitch is similar to the battlement-stitch,
except that the horizontal stitches are made *above* instead of below. It is an arrangement of button-
hole stitches forming a picket-fence or paling, from which it derives its name. Commence by making
a row of button-hole stitches, making the vertical stitches half an inch high and about three-quarters
of an inch apart. Now make a second row, making the vertical stitches one-fourth of an inch to
the right of those in the first row and of the same height. The vertical stitches in the last row are
made at a corresponding distance from those of the second. The stitch may be easily done by
carefully following the directions and illustration.

GROUP OF FANCY BUTTON-HOLE STITCHES.

FIGURES Nos. 1 TO 5.—The ordinary button-hole stitch forms the basis of this group of stitches. The variations are produced by regularly lengthening and shortening the stitches and

FIGURE No. 1.

FIGURE No. 2.

FIGURE No. 3.

FIGURE No. 4.

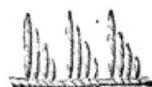

FIGURE No. 5.

by slanting the needle in setting them. Stitches of this description are very pretty for edging blankets, petticoats or any garment which is not to have a hem; or they may be used upon tucks or hemmed edges, or upon bands, etc., etc.

PLAIN AND FANCY CHAIN AND LOOP STITCHES.

While the chain-stitch is perfectly familiar and very simple to make, it and its variations form many pretty decorations for hems, edges, bands, etc., etc. The three engravings seen below per-

FIGURE No. 1.—PLAIN CHAIN-STITCH.

FIGURE No. 2.—TWISTED CHAIN-STITCH.

FIGURE No. 3.—VINE CHAIN-STITCH.

fectly portray as many methods of making it. Figure No. 3, it will be seen, is very like feather-stitching, except that the angle of its stitches is not so acute as that seen in feather-stitching.

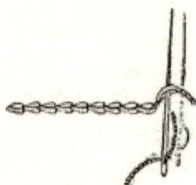

FIGURE No. 4.

At figure No. 4 the split-stitch, which resembles a chain-stitch, is shown. It is worked very much like an outline-stitch except that the point of the needle must pierce right through the center of the thread close to where it came out of the material in each preceding stitch.

The remaining engravings on this page fully explain themselves and may be used according to personal taste and judgment upon such

FIGURE No. 5.

FIGURE No. 6.

FIGURE No. 7.

FIGURE No. 8.

FIGURE No. 9.

garments or parts of garments as may be thus appropriately decorated.

Plain and fancy loop or chain-stitches are pretty made either with silk, cotton, linen or wool working thread, and two tints, shades or colors may be employed in making some of them. At figures Nos. 8 and 10 the engravings show how fancy loop-stitches may be employed in fastening down a hem; and figures Nos. 6 and 9 furnish clear illustrations of the method of making the loop-stitch used at figures Nos. 8 and 10.

FIGURE No. 10.

Cross-Stitch Designs for Decorating Garments made of Plain or Checked Materials.

The cross or plain canvas stitch is very popular for border-embroideries for dresses, aprons, cloaks, blankets or wrappers, and in fact for any garment for which such designs are appropriate.

Upon cotton or wool fabrics of pin-head or shepherd's check designs, the checks form the guide by which the stitches are set, the same as do the checks of canvas; but when a cross-stitch design is to be applied to a garment made of plain fabric, the best plan is to baste along the portion to be embroidered a strip of thin open-meshed canvas, and over it

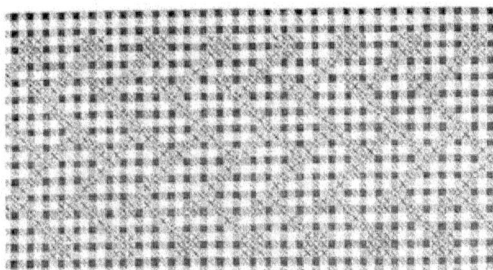

FIGURE No. 1.—CROSS-STITCH EMBROIDERY ON CHECKED MATERIAL.

work the design through the fabric. When the design is worked remove the canvas by carefully drawing out its threads; it will then be found accurately embroidered upon the garment.

Figures Nos. 2 and 3 show how the cross-stitch may be made by two

FIGURE No. 2.—METHOD OF MAKING PLAIN CROSS-STITCH

FIGURE No. 3.—METHOD OF MAKING PERSIAN CROSS-STITCH.

methods, the first being the plain cross-stitch and the second the Persian cross-stitch. At figure No. 4 the star cross-stitch is shown and can be easily followed from the engraving. Instructions for embroidering either cross-stitch upon checked goods are given below.

In embroidering a cross-stitch design upon a checked gingham or wool fabric, the design desired may be reduced or enlarged by the following plan: While one square or tiny block of a checked pattern is generally supposed to represent the space for one cross-stitch, (see figure No. 1) if the checks are small, four, nine or sixteen checks may be used as the space for one stitch; and on this basis the pattern may be increased as much as may be desirable, always keeping a perfect square of the checks for every stitch.

FIGURE No. 4.—STAR CROSS-STITCH.

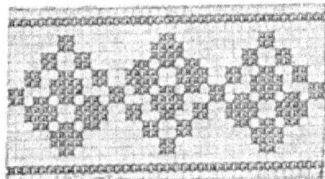

FIGURE No. 5.—CROSS-STITCH DESIGN FOR CHECKED OR PLAIN MATERIAL.

Fine smooth twine, or Dexter's knitting cotton is generally used for decorating garments of wash fabrics such as aprons and house dresses. Finer cottons are used for embroidering children's garments of gingham; but for woollen fabrics, silk is usually chosen for the embroidery thread,

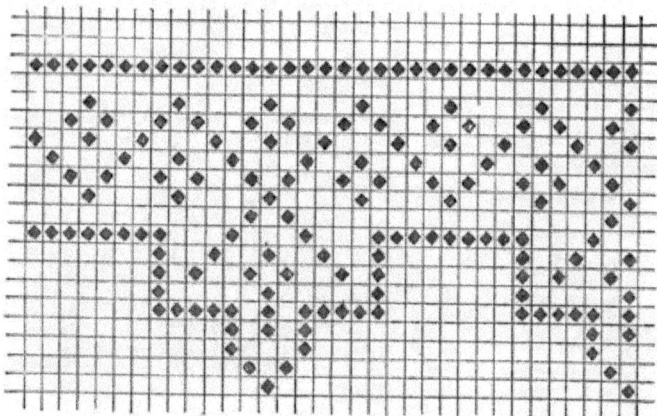

FIGURE No. 6.—CROSS-STITCH DESIGN FOR A SHEPHERD'S CHECK DRESS.

although fine Saxony yarn or crewel is sometimes used for the purpose. Cross-stitching may be very prettily done in one, two or several colors in silks on a baby's blanket, cloak or petticoats.

FIGURE No. 6.—CROSS-STITCH DESIGN FOR A SHEPHERD'S CHECK DRESS.—In this, as in canvas work, the blocks or squares should be counted, and the design, which may be easily followed, is worked in the simple cross-stitch. The color of the cotton or silk used may match or contrast with those in the check. Sometimes the embroidery is done all in one color, and again both colors of the check are introduced. This pattern is especially adapted for plain skirts, and may be reversed to form a broad border on or above the hem. By the exercise of a little care, this design may be worked on a tea-gown in delicate shades of silk, with very effective results.

FIGURE No. 7.—EMBROIDERY DESIGN FOR

FIGURE No. 7.—EMBROIDERY DESIGN FOR GINGHAMS, SMALL CHECKS, ETC.

GINGHAMS, SMALL CHECKS, ETC.—This figure shows an artistic border in fancy stitches for any goods having a similar checked foundation. The border is made in the following manner: Count as many blocks or squares up from the edge of the hem as will look well in proportion to the length

o. the skirt. Bring the needle up from underneath and pass it over the crosswise line of the goods down through the point where the lengthwise line crosses it; then bring it up at the next point of

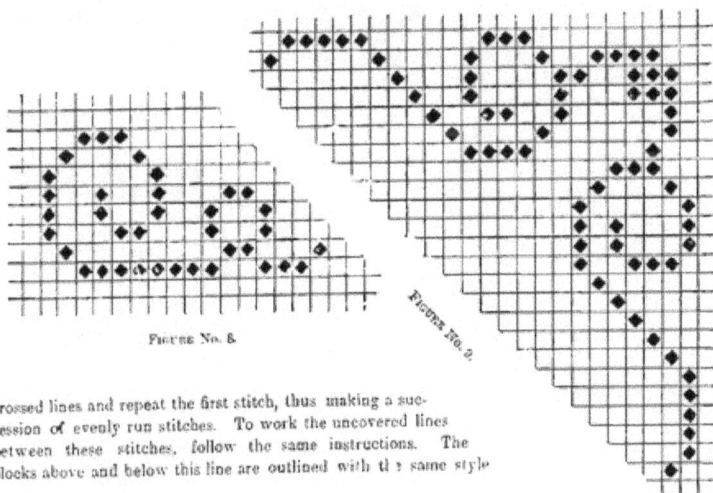

Figure No. 8.

Figure No. 9.

crossed lines and repeat the first stitch, thus making a succession of evenly run stitches. To work the uncovered lines between these stitches, follow the same instructions. The blocks above and below this line are outlined with the same style

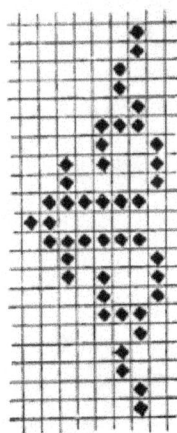

Figure No. 10.

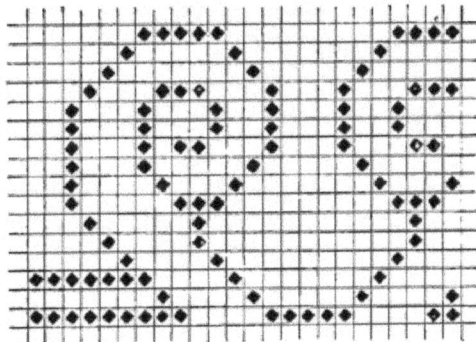

Figure No. 11.

FIGURES Nos. 8, 9, 10 AND 11.—CROSS-STITCH DESIGN FOR SPECIAL PARTS OF LADIES' APRONS

of stitch, and after the first block on each line is completed, skip three blocks and work the fourth square all across the straight line of stitches. The stitches extending from the corners of these squares are made in the same manner, except that they run diagonally through the square.

The remainder of the design may be easily completed by following these directions and carefully counting the squares.

FIGURES NOS. 8, 9, 10, 11.—CROSS-STITCH DESIGN FOR SPECIAL PARTS OF LADIES' APRONS.—This design is especially arranged for aprons, but it may also be used on dresses of gingham, cross-barred muslin and, in fact, on all varieties of checked materials. By counting the squares the design may be easily reproduced. Figure No. 11 shows a section for the border, at figure No. 9 the pocket design may be seen, and figures Nos. 8 and 10 represent designs for the lapels and belt. This stitch may be made in wash silk, cotton or linen in appropriate shades to correspond with the goods.

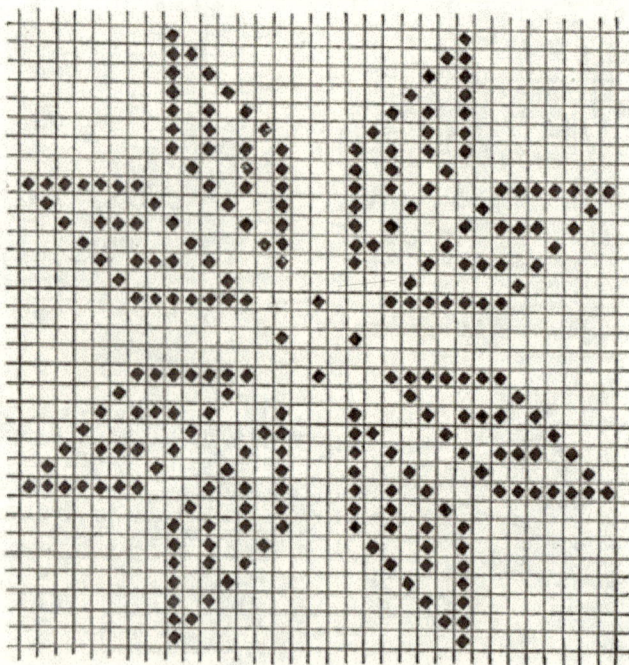

FIGURE NO. 12.—DESIGN FOR EMBROIDERING MISSES' APRONS.

FIGURE NO. 12.—DESIGN FOR EMBROIDERING MISSES' APRONS.—An apron decorated by this design will be pretty and protective to wear during lessons at the cooking school, or by the artist in her studio or the busy little housekeeper. It should be of the regulation long-sleeved, high-necked sack style and may entirely cover the dress. The decoration is done around the bottom and on the pockets in cross-stitch, and the correct size of the design is represented at figure No. 12. The material may be white or colored and of a plain or fancy variety, as preferred, the decoration being very easy of execution on checked goods. Gingham, seersucker, chambray, muslin, linen, checks and all apron materials will be appropriate. The embroidery may be done in one or more colors, if desired.

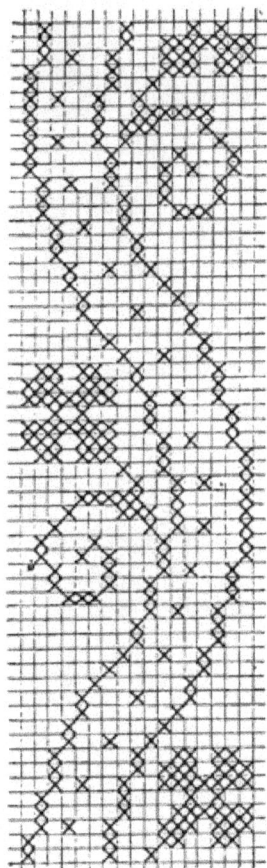

FIGURE No. 13.—DESIGN IN CROSS-STITCH.

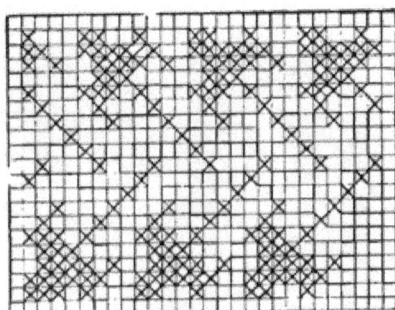

FIGURE No. 14.

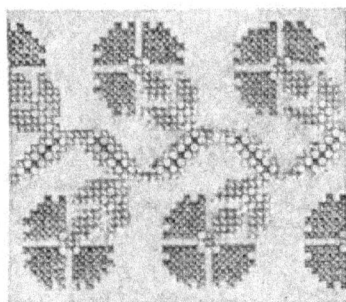

FIGURE No. 15.

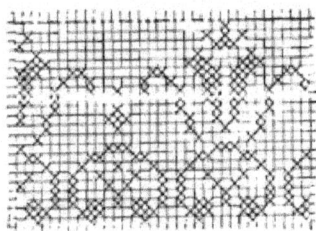

FIGURE No. 16.

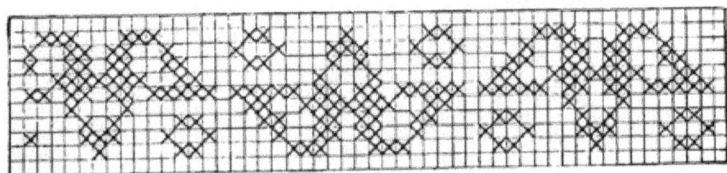

FIGURE No. 17.

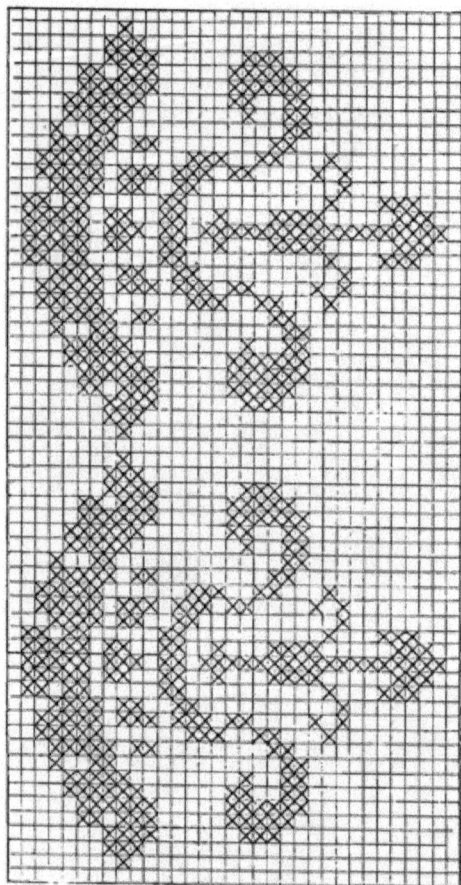

FIGURE No. 18.

FIGURE No. 20.

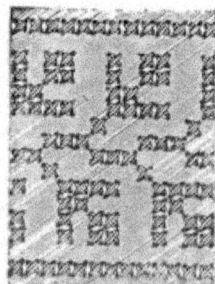

FIGURE No. 19.

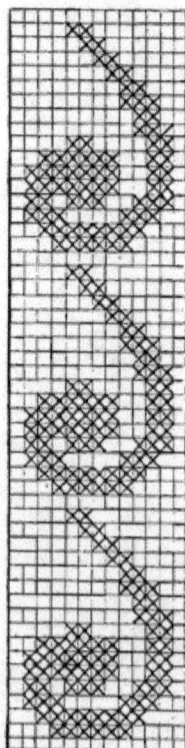

FIGURE No. 21.

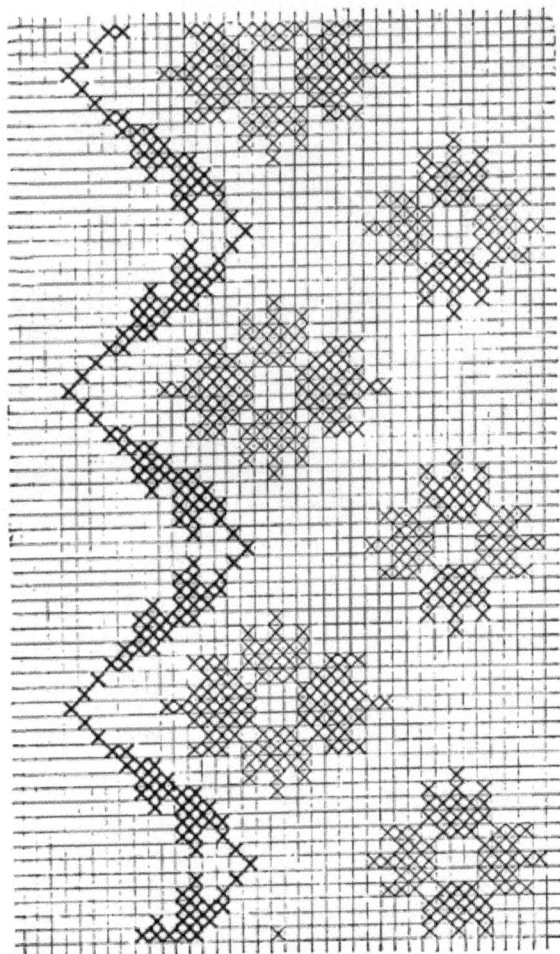

Figure No. 22.

DESIGNS FOR CORNERS OF GARMENTS.

The designs given on this page are suitable for the decoration of any garments requiring borders which include corners. They may also be used for blankets, robes, spreads or any article of a like

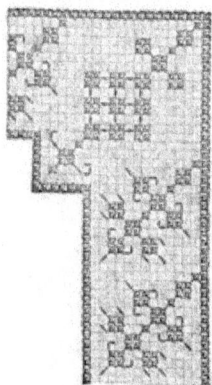

FIGURE No. 1.

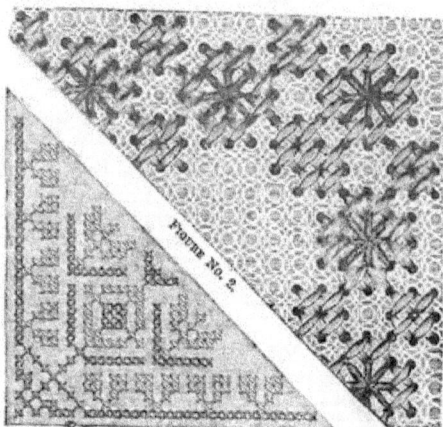

FIGURE No. 3.

nature. They are appropriate for plain or checked goods and may be applied in the sizes illus-

FIGURE No. 4.

FIGURE No. 5.

trated, or enlarged according to the suggestions previously given for getting each stitch within a certain number of checks ranging from one to sixteen for each square.

DESIGNS FOR CORNERS AND SECTIONS OF GARMENTS.

The designs here presented very well explain their own purposes. They are appropriate for the ornamentation of corners whose edges are followed by some pretty border which

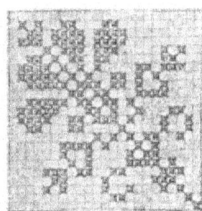

FIGURE No. 1.

FIGURE No. 2.

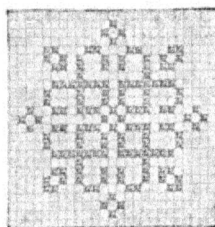

FIGURE No. 3.

FIGURE No. 4.

FIGURE No. 5.

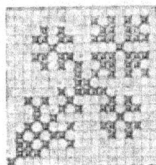

FIGURE No. 6.

FIGURE No. 7.

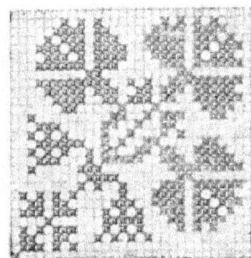

FIGURE No. 8.

does not include its own also suitable for any requiring a separate or collars, cuffs, laps, and the girdles, pockets, etc., etc. suitable for the pur- may also be used for scarfs, bracket - lambre- household belonging re- this description. When suggested, these designs colors, and very often in corner design ; and are sections of a garment namentation, such as col- ends of tabs, ties, belts, While these designs are poses mentioned, they the decoration of tidies, quins, mats or any little quiring a decoration of used for the purposes are developed in fancy black or brown.

DESIGNS FOR FILLING IN CHECKS AND MAKING BORDERS.

It will be observed that the engravings given on this page represent designs that may entirely cover a section of a garment, or be used as a border which may consist of as many rows of the

FIGURE No. 1.

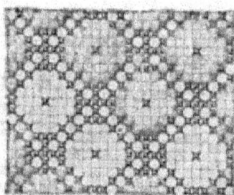

FIGURE No. 2.

FIGURE No. 3.

FIGURE No. 4.

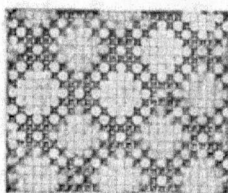

FIGURE No. 6.

FIGURE No. 7.

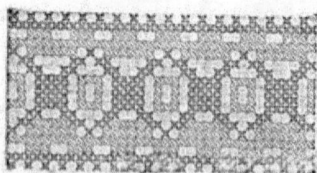

FIGURE No. 5.

FIGURE No. 8.

cross-stitching as may be desired. White, black or colors in either silk or wool may be used in developing either design given, according to the garment and the fabric chosen for it.

DESIGNS FOR EDGINGS AND HEADINGS.

The pointed designs upon this page are very pretty for the decoration of flannel petticoats for children or adults. The work is completed along a plain edge and the latter is afterward cut away. In the design seen at figure No. 1, the open-work must be very carefully cut out or the work will

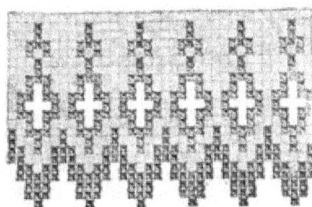

FIGURE No. 1.

FIGURE No. 2.

FIGURE No. 3.

FIGURE No. 4.

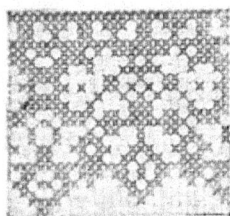

FIGURE No. 5.

FIGURE No. 6.

FIGURE No. 7.

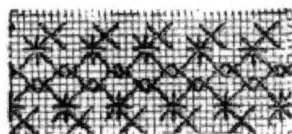

FIGURE No. 8.

FIGURE No. 9.

FIGURE No. 10.

fray. If preferred, its edges may be left as seen at figure No. 3; and the same is true of figure No. 6. The headings represented may or may not be used in connection with the edgings. They are pretty by themselves, when added above tucks or ruffles. Red, blue, yellow, pink, brown or black silk, crewel or working cotton is generally used in developing whichever design may be selected.

DESIGNS FOR BANDS, BORDERS, ETC.

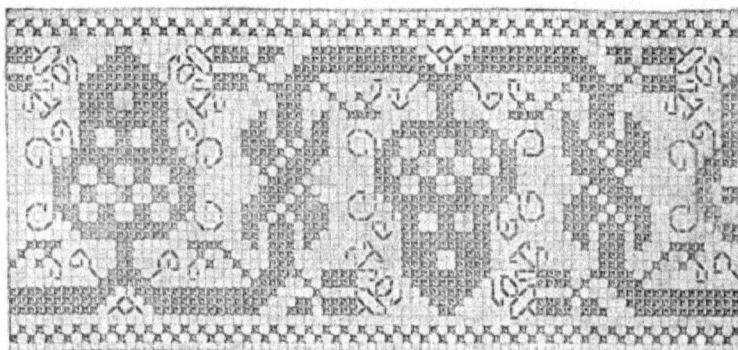

FIGURE No. 1.

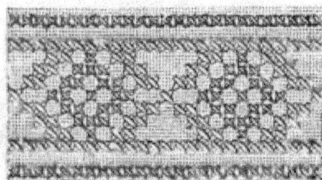

FIGURE No. 2.

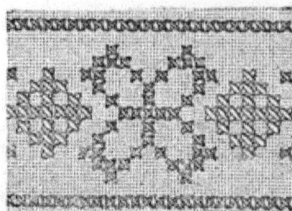

FIGURE No. 3.

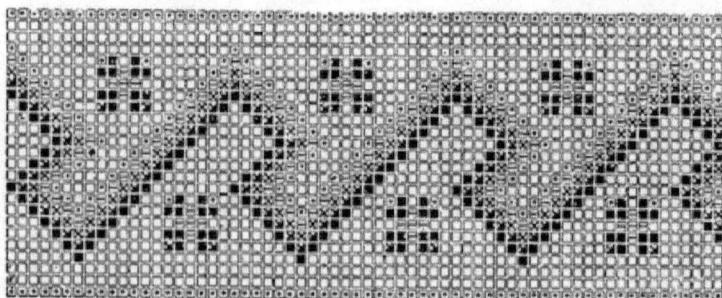

FIGURE No. 4.

FIGURE No. 5

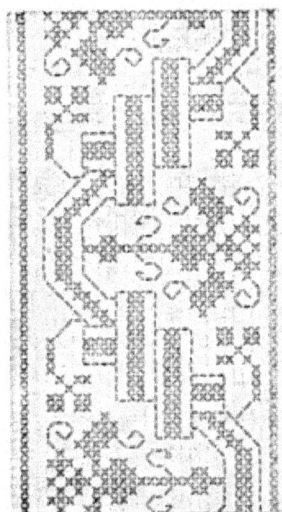

FIGURE No. 6.

FIGURE No. 7.

FIGURE No. 8.

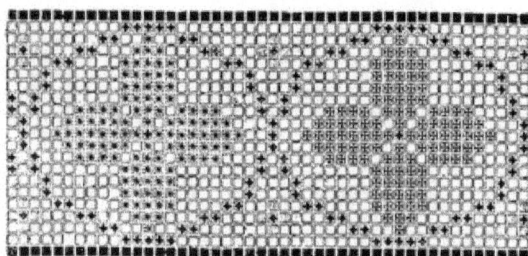

FIGURE No. 9.

FIGURE No. 10.

FIGURE No. 11.

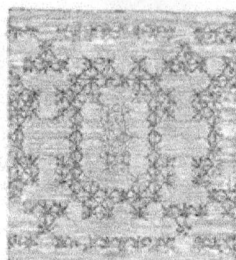

FIGURE No. 12.

FIGURE No. 13.

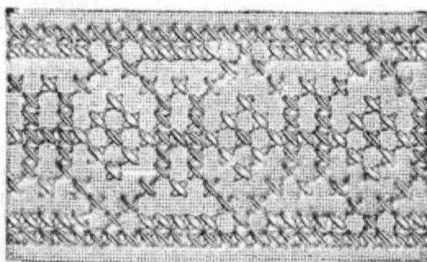

FIGURE No. 14.

FIGURE No. 15.

FIGURE No. 16.

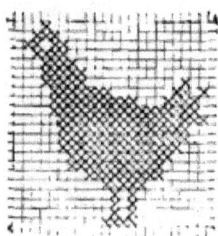

FIGURE NO. 17.

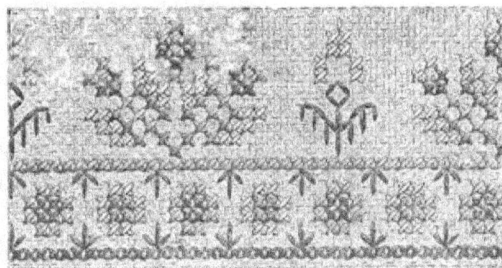

FIGURE NO. 18.

FIGURE NO. 19.

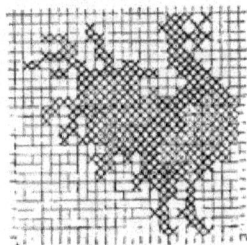

FIGURE NO. 20.

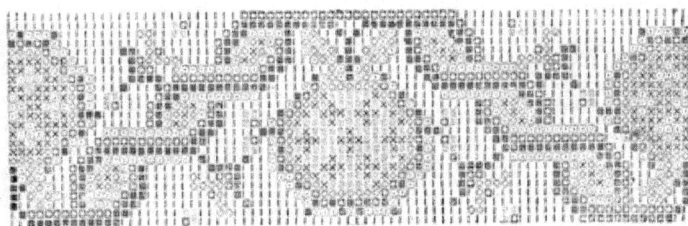

FIGURE NO. 21.

FIGURE NO. 22.

FIGURE NO. 23.

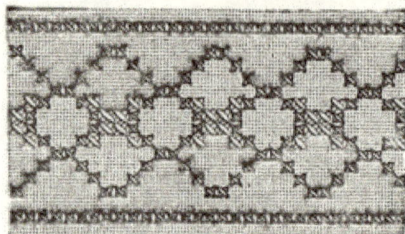

FIGURE NO. 24.

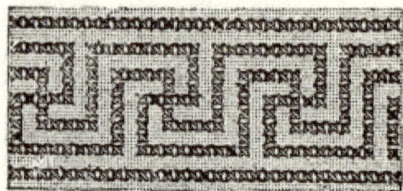

FIGURE NO. 25.

FIGURE NO. 26.

FIGURE NO. 27.

FIGURE NO 28.

FIGURE NO. 29.

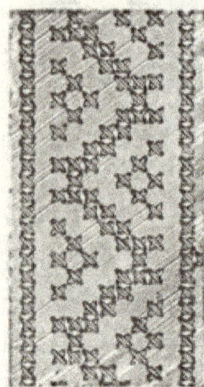

FIGURE NO. 30.

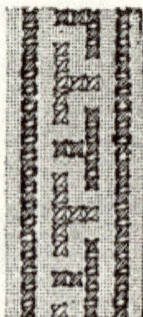

FIGURE NO. 31.

FIGURE NO. 32.

FIGURE NO. 33.

Designs for Darned Net, Scarfs, Kerchiefs, Tidies, Edgings, Insertions, etc.

Bobbin net, or "bobbinet," or "net" as it is now commonly called, was first made by machinery in 1809, and was so called because the threads from which it was made were wound upon bobbins,

Figure No. 1.—Pillow-Sham of Darned Net.

and *twisted* into meshes instead of being *looped* in knitting style as they were previous to the invention of the machine. The latter was invented by John Heathcoat, the son of an English farmer;

FIGURE No. 2.—SECTION OF PILLOW-SHAM.

or, the design may be drawn on thick paper and the net basted over it; or, if the net is coarse the design may be followed by counting the meshes and inserting the needle and floss accordingly; or the design may be transferred to the net itself by black or colored pencils, or stamping. The darner must decide for herself which method of holding the work she will use. Some of the most expert darners simply hold the net loosely in their hands and copy the design by eye alone. Wash-silk floss, India floss which is of linen but looks like silk, and ordinary darning flosses are all used for this work. Darned net is liked for many purposes, as will be observed by the variety of designs and illustrations given.

but to France must be given the credit of introducing the "darned work" by which some of its costliest net laces were first made. From these laces originated the industry of darning net by machinery and by hand, and in all grades from fine silk-blonde and Brussels net to the coarsest wash net, such as is used for curtains and draperies.

In the earlier days the pattern was stamped on the net by means of wooden blocks, and the net was then placed in a frame, and the darner with her left hand under the lace followed the design with her needle and cotton, linen or silk floss held over the work in the right hand. This method may be employed at the present time;

FIGURE No. 3.—SECTION OF PILLOW-SHAM.

FIGURE No. 4.—CENTER OF PILLOW-SHAM.

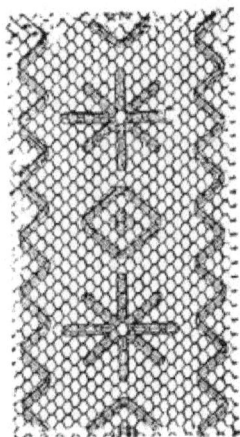

FIGURE No. 5.—DARNED-NET EDGING.

FIGURE No. 6.—SECTION OF PILLOW-SHAM.

FIGURE No. 7.—DARNED-NET EDGING.

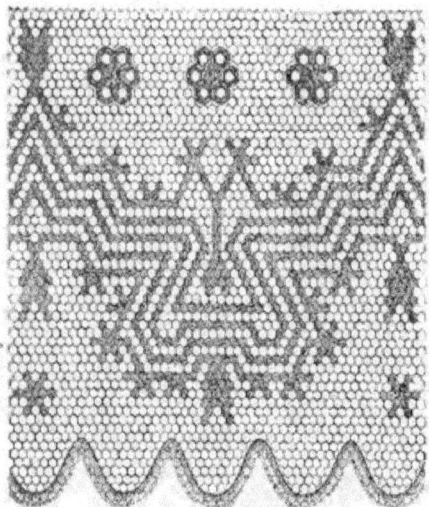

FIGURE NO. 8.—EDGING IN DARNED NET.

FIGURE NO. 9.—DESIGN IN DARNED NET.

FIGURE NO. 10.—EDGING OF DARNED NET.

FIGURE No. 11.—TIE-END OF DARNED NET (FULL WIDTH).

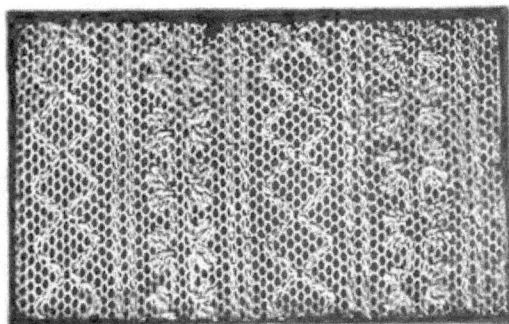

FIGURE No. 12.—DESIGN FOR A YOKE OR SECTION OF A GARMENT IN DARNED NET.

FIGURE No. 13.—TIDY OF DARNED NET.

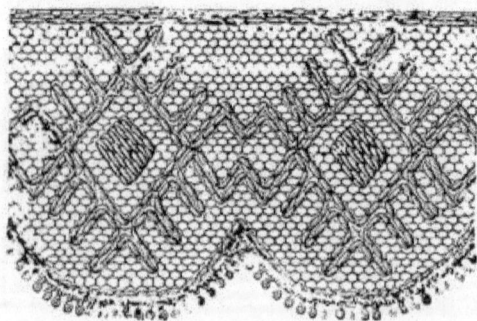

FIGURE No. 14.—DESIGN FOR DARNED NET.

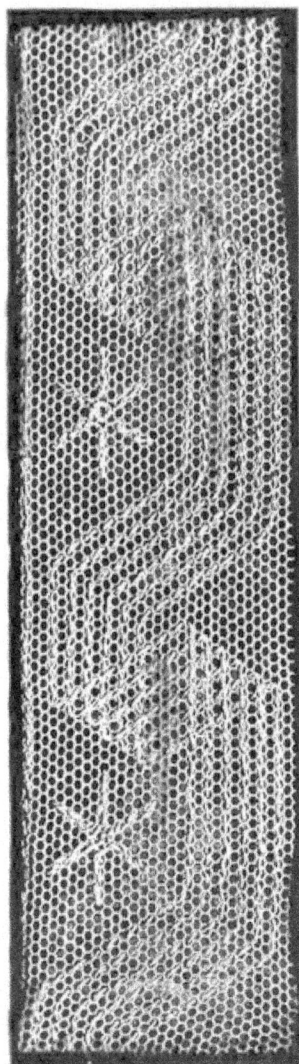

FIGURE NO. 16.—BORDER FOR DARNED NET.

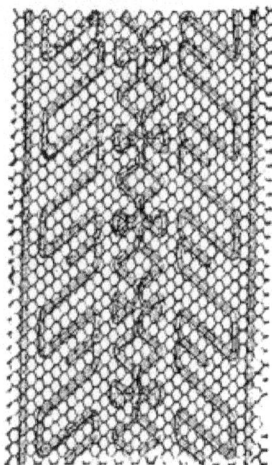

FIGURE NO. 15.—DESIGN FOR DARNED NET.

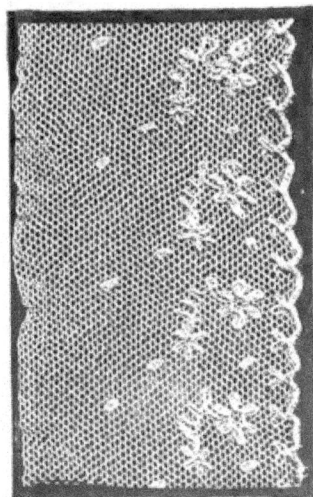

FIGURE NO. 17.—EDGING OF DARNED NET.

FIGURE No. 18.—CORNER OF KERCHIEF OF DARNED NET (HALF SIZE).

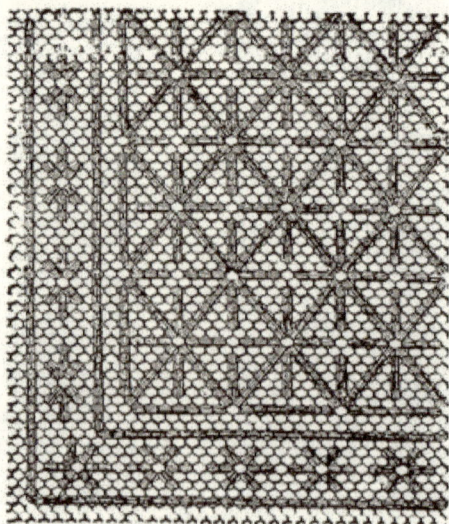

FIGURE No. 19.—DESIGN FOR A CORNER OR SQUARE OF DARNED NET.

FIGURE No. 20.—SCARF-END OF DARNED NET (HALF SIZE).

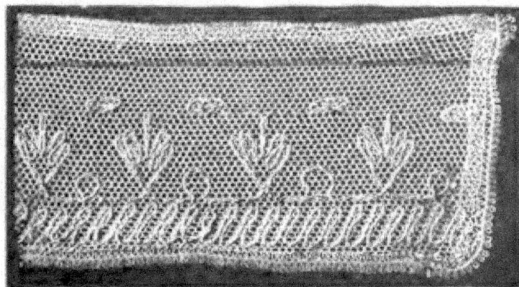

FIGURE No. 21.—NARROW CUFF OF DARNED NET.

FIGURE NO. 22.—DARNED NET-EDGING, WITH OVERWROUGHT STITCH (FULL SIZE).

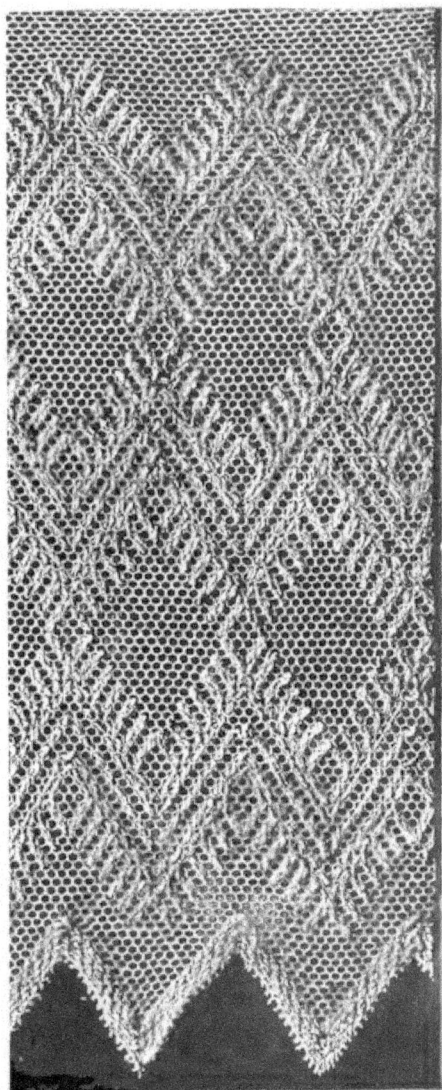

Figure No. 25.—Design for Darned Net.

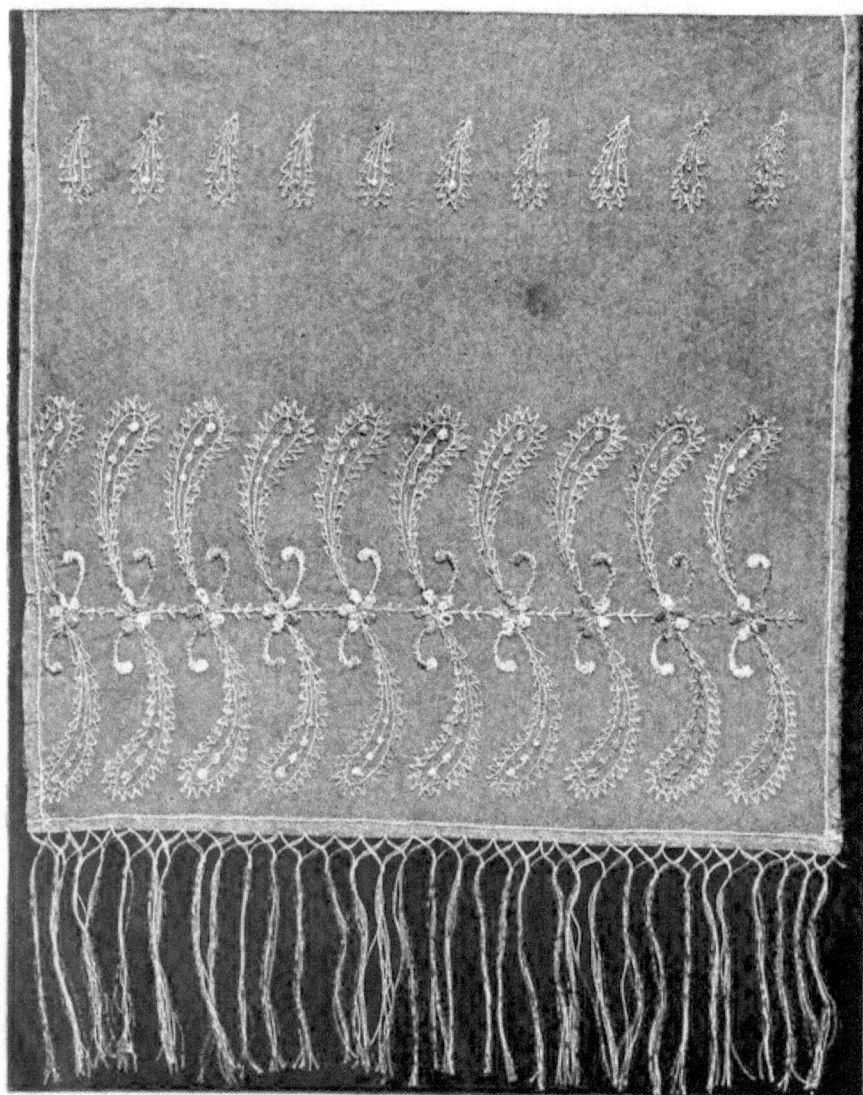

FIGURE No. 24.—PAISLEY SCARF.

FIGURE NO. 25.—CORNER OF TIDY IN DARNED NET.

FIGURE NO. 26.—DESIGN FOR DARNED NET.

FIGURE NO. 27.—DESIGN FOR DARNED NET.

FIGURE No. 28.—CORNER AND BORDER-DESIGN FOR DARNED NET.

FIGURE No. 29.—STRIPE IN DARNED NET.

FIGURE No. 30.—DESIGN FOR EDGING.

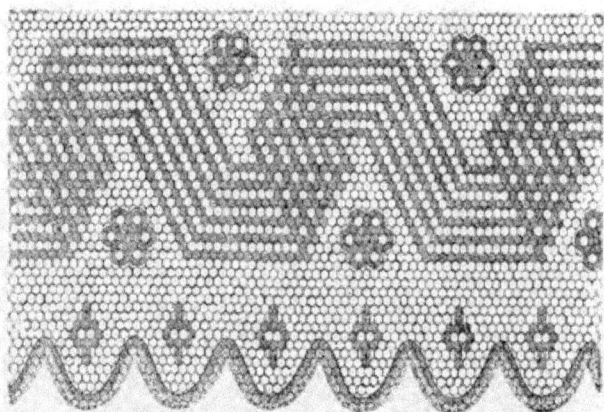

FIGURE No. 31.—DESIGN FOR DARNED-NET EDGING.

FIGURE No. 32.—INSERTION IN DARNED NET.

FIGURE No. 33.—LEAP-SPOT FOR DARNED NET.

FIGURE NO. 34.—END OF DRAPERY-SCARF FOR DARNED NET.

METROPOLITAN PAMPHLET SERIES.

SMOCKING, FANCY STITCHES, AND CROSS-STITCH AND DARNED NET DESIGNS: A Pamphlet, which includes all the Varieties of Needlework mentioned. One of the most important subjects is that of Finishing Seam Ends, Pockets, Pocket-Laps, Collars, Cuffs, etc., by the Tailors' Method. *Price, 6d. (by post, 7½d.) or 15 Cents.*

MOTHER AND BABE: Devoted to the Comfort and Care of Mother and Babe, containing full information concerning the Proper Care of Infants and the preparation of their Wardrobes. Also Treating of the Health, Comfort and Care of the Expectant Mother, and the Proper Clothing for Ladies in Delicate Health. *Price, 6d. (by post, 7½d.) or 15 Cents.*

THE PERFECT ART OF CANNING AND PRESERVING: Explanatory of Canning and Preserving, and containing full instructions regarding Jams, Marmalades, Jellies, Preserves, Canning (including Corn, Peas, Beans, Tomatoes, Asparagus, etc.), Pickling, Catsups, Relishes, etc. *Price, 6d. (by post, 7½d.) or 15 Cents.*

THE CORRECT ART OF CANDY-MAKING: Filled with instructions for French and Domestic Candy-Making, and divided into Departments, which include Cream Candies, Bonbons, Nut and Fruit Candies, Pastes, Drops, Medicated Lozenges, and Candied Fruits, Flowers and Nuts. *Price, 6d. (by post, 7½d.) or 15 Cents.*

DAINTY DESSERTS: In this Pamphlet are directions for the preparation of Dainties adapted to the palate of the epicure or the laborer, with numberless recipes for Puddings, Sauces, Pies, Creams, Custards, and French, Fancy and Frozen Desserts, etc. *Price, 6d. (by post, 7½d.) or 15 Cents.*

EXTRACTS AND BEVERAGES: The Preparation of Syrups, Refreshing Beverages, Colognes, Perfumes, and Various Toilette Accessories, invaluable alike to the Belle and the Housekeeper. *Price, 6d. (by post, 7½d.) or 15 Cents.*

NURSING AND NOURISHMENT FOR INVALIDS: A Pamphlet which places within the reach of everyone interested in Caring for Invalids, Explicit Instructions and Valuable Advice regarding the Best Methods and Necessary Adjuncts in the Sick Room. *Price, 6d. (by post, 7½d.) or 15 Cents.*

BIRDS AND BIRD-KEEPING: Illustrated with Cage-Birds, Cages and Modern Appliances for Cages; accompanied by full instructions for the Care, Food, Management, Breeding, and Treatment of diseases of Songsters and other Feathered Pets. *Price, 6d. (by post, 7½d.) or 15 Cents.*

BEES AND BEE-KEEPING: This Pamphlet is profusely Illustrated, and Treats of the Details necessary to successful Bee-Keeping, whether conducted by the Amateur or advanced Apiarist. *Price, 6d. (by post, 7½d.) or 15 Cents.*

TABLEAUX, CHARADES AND CONUNDRUMS is a Pamphlet upon this class of Entertainments and Amusements. Charades in all their different varieties, and Tableaux are Fully Illustrated and Discussed. The Department devoted to Conundrums is Overflowing with Wit and Merriment. *Price, 6d. (by post, 7½d.) or 15 Cents.*

FANCY DRILLS FOR EVENING ENTERTAINMENTS: A Pamphlet containing Directions and illustrations for the Arrangement and Production of Twelve New Fancy Drills, suitable for School, Church, Club and Society Entertainments. *Price, 6d. (by post, 7½d.) or 15 Cents.*

THE PERFECT ART OF MODERN DANCING: This Pamphlet contains Illustrated Instructions for those who wish to Learn to Dance by the Methods Employed by the Best Dancing Masters of the Metropolis. *Price, 6d. (by post, 7½d.) or 15 Cents.*

WEDDINGS AND WEDDING ANNIVERSARIES: A Pamphlet which is invaluable to Maids and Matrons, Bachelors and Benedicts, and the Bride and Groom Elect. It contains full information concerning the Etiquette of Weddings, and describes all the Anniversaries. *Price, 6d. (by post, 7½d.) or 15 Cts.*

A MANUAL OF LAWN TENNIS: This Pamphlet is adapted to the requirements of Amateur and Professional Players of Tennis. It is fully Illustrated and contains a History of Tennis, the Rules, Details Concerning the Development of Play, Descriptions of the Court, etc. *Price, 6d. (by post, 7½d.) or 15 Cents.*

USES OF CRÊPE AND TISSUE PAPER: This Pamphlet is Illustrated with Designs and Diagrams for Making Paper Flowers and various Fancy Articles, Christmas, Easter and General Gifts, Novelties for Fairs, etc. A child can follow the directions given. *Price, 6d. (by post, 7½d.) or 15 Cents.*

CHILD LIFE: This Pamphlet discusses Influences on Prenatal Life; Bathing and Clothing for Infants; Food for Infants; Weaning and Feeding Children after the First Year; Diseases of Infants and Young Children; Eruptive and Other Fevers; Care of Children's Eyes, Ears and Teeth. *Price, 6d. (by post, 7½d.) or 15 Cents.*

DOGS, CATS AND OTHER PETS: A Pamphlet about pet animals and combines both practical information about their habits, accomplishments and needs, and the sentimental and anecdotical side of the subject. It tells all about the various breeds of dogs. Then these chapters on pet monkeys, squirrel, rabbits, rats, mice, pigeons, crows, frogs, chameleons, tortoises, etc. *Price, 6d. (by post, 7½d.) or 15 Cents.*

HEALTH: HOW TO BE WELL AND LIVE LONG: The Special Mission of this Pamphlet is fully indicated by its sub-title. Rational Personal Care of One's Natural Physical Condition, without the Aid of Drugs and Medicines, except when the latter are absolutely necessary, are two of the many strong points of the subject matter of the Pamphlet. *Price, 6d. (by post 7½d.) or 15 Cents.*

BURNT WORK: Full instructions for the popular art of Burnt Work, together with Illustrations of Implements, Methods and Designs appear in this pamphlet, rendering it a most valuable manual among the many others devoted to art. Its details can be applied to various Useful and Decorative purposes, from Portraits to Furniture, from Dainty Toilette Articles to Panels. No artist or lover of art, amateur or professional, should fail to send for a copy of the pamphlet. *Price, 6d. (by post, 7½d.) or 15 Cents.*

PLEASE NOTE.—We will send any of the above Pamphlets to any Address on receipt of Price.

THE BUTTERICK PUBLISHING CO. (Limited),

171 to 175, Regent Street, London, W.; or 7 to 17 West 13th Street, New York.